GITANJALI

GITANJALI

(SONG OFFERINGS)

BY

RABINDRANATH TAGORE

A COLLECTION OF PROSE TRANSLATIONS
MADE BY THE AUTHOR FROM
THE ORIGINAL BENGALI

WITH AN INTRODUCTION BY
W. B. YEATS

LONDON
MACMILLAN & CO LTD
NEW YORK · ST MARTIN'S PRESS
1959

*This book is copyright in all countries which
are signatories to the Berne Convention*

—

*Formerly issued (1912) in a limited Edition by the Indian Society
First published by Macmillan & Co. March 1913
Macmillan's Pocket Library 1949
Reprinted 1951, 1953, 1957, 1959*

MACMILLAN AND COMPANY LIMITED
London Bombay Calcutta Madras Melbourne

THE MACMILLAN COMPANY OF CANADA LIMITED
Toronto

ST MARTIN'S PRESS INC
New York

TO

WILLIAM ROTHENSTEIN

INTRODUCTION

A FEW days ago I said to a distinguished
Bengali doctor of medicine, " I know no
German, yet if a translation of a Ger-
man poet had moved me, I would go
to the British Museum and find books
in English that would tell me some-
thing of his life, and of the history of
his thought. But though these prose
translations from Rabindranath Tagore
have stirred my blood as nothing has
for years, I shall not know anything
of his life, and of the movements of
thought that have made them possible,
if some Indian traveller will not tell
me." It seemed to him natural that I
should be moved, for he said, " I read

Rabindranath every day, to read one
line of his is to forget all the troubles
of the world." I said, "An Englishman
living in London in the reign of Richard
the Second had he been shown trans-
lations from Petrarch or from Dante,
would have found no books to answer
his questions, but would have questioned
some Florentine banker or Lombard
merchant as I question you. For all I
know, so abundant and simple is this
poetry, the new Renaissance has been
born in your country and I shall never
know of it except by hearsay." He
answered, "We have other poets, but
none that are his equal ; we call this
the epoch of Rabindranath. No poet
seems to me as famous in Europe as
he is among us. He is as great in
music as in poetry, and his songs are
sung from the west of India into Bur-
mah wherever Bengali is spoken. He
was already famous at nineteen when

he wrote his first novel; and plays, written when he was but little older, are still played in Calcutta. I so much admire the completeness of his life; when he was very young he wrote much of natural objects, he would sit all day in his garden; from his twenty-fifth year or so to his thirty-fifth perhaps, when he had a great sorrow, he wrote the most beautiful love poetry in our language"; and then he said with deep emotion, "words can never express what I owed at seventeen to his love poetry. After that his art grew deeper, it became religious and philosophical; all the aspirations of mankind are in his hymns. He is the first among our saints who has not refused to live, but has spoken out of Life itself, and that is why we give him our love." I may have changed his well-chosen words in my memory but not his thought. "A little while ago he

was to read divine service in one of
our churches—we of the Brahma Samaj
use your word 'church' in English—it
was the largest in Calcutta and not
only was it crowded, people even stand-
ing in the windows, but the streets
were all but impassable because of the
people."

Other Indians came to see me and
their reverence for this man sounded
strange in our world, where we hide
great and little things under the same
veil of obvious comedy and half-serious
depreciation.   When we were making
the cathedrals had we a like reverence
for our great men ?   "Every morning
at three—I know, for I have seen it "—
one said to me, "he sits immovable in
contemplation, and for two hours does
not awake from his reverie upon the
nature of God. His father, the Maha
Rishi, would sometimes sit there all
through the next day ; once, upon a

river, he fell into contemplation because
of the beauty of the landscape, and the
rowers waited for eight hours before
they could continue their journey." He
then told me of Mr. Tagore's family
and how for generations great men
have come out of its cradles. "To-
day," he said, "there are Gogonen-
dranath and Abanindranath Tagore,
who are artists; and Dwijendranath,
Rabindranath's brother, who is a great
philosopher. The squirrels come from
the boughs and climb on to his knees
and the birds alight upon his hands."
I notice in these men's thought a sense
of visible beauty and meaning as though
they held that doctrine of Nietzsche
that we must not believe in the moral
or intellectual beauty which does not
sooner or later impress itself upon
physical things. I said, "In the East
you know how to keep a family illustri-
ous. The other day the curator of a

Museum pointed out to me a little
dark-skinned man who was arranging
their Chinese prints and said, ' That
is the hereditary connoisseur of the
Mikado, he is the fourteenth of his
family to hold the post.' "   He
answered. " When Rabindranath was a
boy he had all round him in his home
literature and music." I thought of
the abundance, of the simplicity of the
poems, and said, " In your country is
there much propagandist writing, much
criticism ? We have to do so much,
especially in my own country, that our
minds gradually cease to be creative,
and yet we cannot help it. If our life
was not a continual warfare, we would
not have taste, we would not know
what is good, we would not find hearers
and readers. Four-fifths of our energy
is spent in the quarrel with bad taste,
whether in our own minds or in the
minds of others." " I understand," he

replied, "we too have our propagandist writing. In the villages they recite long mythological poems adapted from the Sanscrit in the Middle Ages, and they often insert passages telling the people that they must do their duties."

II

I have carried the manuscript of these translations about with me for days, reading it in railway trains, or on the top of omnibuses and in restaurants, and I have often had to close it lest some stranger would see how much it moved me. These lyrics— which are in the original, my Indians tell me, full of subtlety of rhythm, of untranslatable delicacies of colour, of metrical invention — display in their thought a world I have dreamed of all my life long. The work of a supreme culture, they yet appear as

much the growth of the common soil
as the grass and the rushes. A tradi-
tion, where poetry and religion are
the same thing, has passed through the
centuries, gathering from learned and
unlearned metaphor and emotion, and
carried back again to the multitude
the thought of the scholar and of the
noble. If the civilization of Bengal
remains unbroken, if that common
mind which — as one divines — runs
through all, is not, as with us, broken
into a dozen minds that know nothing
of each other, something even of what
is most subtle in these verses will have
come, in a few generations, to the
beggar on the roads. When there
was but one mind in England Chaucer
wrote his *Troilus and Cressida*, and
though he had written to be read, or
to be read out — for our time was
coming on apace — he was sung by
minstrels for a while. Rabindranath

Tagore, like Chaucer's forerunners, writes music for his words, and one understands at every moment that he is so abundant, so spontaneous, so daring in his passion, so full of surprise, because he is doing something which has never seemed strange, unnatural, or in need of defence. These verses will not lie in little well-printed books upon ladies' tables, who turn the pages with indolent hands that they may sigh over a life without meaning, which is yet all they can know of life, or be carried about by students at the university to be laid aside when the work of life begins, but as the generations pass, travellers will hum them on the highway and men rowing upon rivers. Lovers, while they await one another, shall find, in murmuring them, this love of God a magic gulf wherein their own more bitter passion may bathe and renew its youth. At every

B

moment the heart of this poet flows
outward to these without derogation or
condescension, for it has known that
they will understand ; and it has filled
itself with the circumstance of their
lives. The traveller in the red-brown
clothes that he wears that dust may
not show upon him, the girl searching
in her bed for the petals fallen from
the wreath of her royal lover, the
servant or the bride awaiting the
master's home - coming in the empty
house, are images of the heart turning
to God. Flowers and rivers, the
blowing of conch shells, the heavy rain
of the Indian July, or the parching
heat, are images of the moods of that
heart in union or in separation ; and
a man sitting in a boat upon a river
playing upon a lute, like one of those
figures full of mysterious meaning in
a Chinese picture, is God Himself.
A whole people, a whole civilization,

immeasurably strange to us, seems to have been taken up into this imagination; and yet we are not moved because of its strangeness, but because we have met our own image, as though we had walked in Rossetti's willow wood, or heard, perhaps for the first time in literature, our voice as in a dream.

Since the Renaissance the writing of European saints—however familiar their metaphor and the general structure of their thought—has ceased to hold our attention. We know that we must at last forsake the world, and we are accustomed in moments of weariness or exaltation to consider a voluntary forsaking; but how can we, who have read so much poetry, seen so many paintings, listened to so much music, where the cry of the flesh and the cry of the soul seem one, forsake it harshly and rudely? What have we in common

with St. Bernard covering his eyes that
they may not dwell upon the beauty of
the lakes of Switzerland, or with the
violent rhetoric of the Book of Revela-
tion? We would, if we might, find,
as in this book, words full of courtesy.
" I have got my leave. Bid me fare-
well, my brothers! I bow to you all
and take my departure. Here I give
back the keys of my door—and I give
up all claims to my house. I only ask
for last kind words from you. We
were neighbours for long, but I received
more than I could give. Now the day
has dawned and the lamp that lit my
dark corner is out. A summons has
come and I am ready for my journey."
And it is our own mood, when it is
furthest from À Kempis or John of the
Cross, that cries, " And because I love
this life, I know I shall love death
as well." Yet it is not only in our
thoughts of the parting that this book

fathoms all. We had not known that
we loved God, hardly it may be that
we believed in Him ; yet looking back-
ward upon our life we discover, in our
exploration of the pathways of woods,
in our delight in the lonely places of
hills, in that mysterious claim that we
have made, unavailingly, on the women
that we have loved, the emotion
that created this insidious sweetness.
"Entering my heart unbidden even
as one of the common crowd, unknown
to me, my king, thou didst press the
signet of eternity upon many a fleet-
ing moment." This is no longer the
sanctity of the cell and of the scourge ;
being but a lifting up, as it were, into a
greater intensity of the mood of the
painter, painting the dust and the sun-
light, and we go for a like voice to St.
Francis and to William Blake who
have seemed so alien in our violent
history.

III

We write long books where no
page perhaps has any quality to make
writing a pleasure, being confident in
some general design, just as we fight
and make money and fill our heads
with politics—all dull things in the
doing — while Mr. Tagore, like the
Indian civilization itself, has been con-
tent to discover the soul and surrender
himself to its spontaneity. He often
seems to contrast his life with that of
those who have lived more after our
fashion, and have more seeming weight
in the world, and always humbly as
though he were only sure his way is
best for him: "Men going home glance
at me and smile and fill me with
shame. I sit like a beggar maid, draw-
ing my skirt over my face, and when
they ask me, what it is I want, I drop

my eyes and answer them not." At
another time, remembering how his life
had once a different shape, he will say,
"Many an hour have I spent in the
strife of the good and the evil, but now
it is the pleasure of my playmate of
the empty days to draw my heart on
to him; and I know not why is this
sudden call to what useless inconse-
quence." An innocence, a simplicity
that one does not find elsewhere in
literature makes the birds and the
leaves seem as near to him as they are
near to children, and the changes of
the seasons great events as before our
thoughts had arisen between them and
us. At times I wonder if he has it
from the literature of Bengal or from
religion, and at other times, remember-
ing the birds alighting on his brother's
hands, I find pleasure in thinking it
hereditary, a mystery that was growing
through the centuries like the courtesy

of a Tristan or a Pelanore. Indeed, when he is speaking of children, so much a part of himself this quality seems, one is not certain that he is not also speaking of the saints, " They build their houses with sand and they play with empty shells. With withered leaves they weave their boats and smilingly float them on the vast deep. Children have their play on the seashore of worlds. They know not how to swim, they know not how to cast nets. Pearl fishers dive for pearls, merchants sail in their ships, while children gather pebbles and scatter them again. They seek not for hidden treasures, they know not how to cast nets."

W. B. YEATS.

September **1912.**

1

Thou hast made me endless, such is thy pleasure. This frail vessel thou emptiest again and again, and fillest it ever with fresh life.

This little flute of a reed thou hast carried over hills and dales, and hast breathed through it melodies eternally new.

At the immortal touch of thy hands my little heart loses its limits in joy and gives birth to utterance ineffable.

Thy infinite gifts come to me only on these very small hands of mine. Ages pass, and still thou pourest, and still there is room to fill.

2

WHEN thou commandest me to sing it seems that my heart would break with pride ; and I look to thy face, and tears come to my eyes.

All that is harsh and dissonant in my life melts into one sweet harmony —and my adoration spreads wings like a glad bird on its flight across the sea.

I know thou takest pleasure in my singing. I know that only as a singer I come before thy presence.

I touch by the edge of the far spreading wing of my song thy feet which I could never aspire to reach.

Drunk with the joy of singing I forget myself and call thee friend who art my lord.

3

I KNOW not how thou singest, my master! I ever listen in silent amazement.

The light of thy music illumines the world. The life breath of thy music runs from sky to sky. The holy stream of thy music breaks through all stony obstacles and rushes on.

My heart longs to join in thy song, but vainly struggles for a voice. I would speak, but speech breaks not into song, and I cry out baffled. Ah, thou hast made my heart captive in the endless meshes of thy music, my master!

4

LIFE of my life, I shall ever try to keep my body pure, knowing that thy living touch is upon all my limbs.

I shall ever try to keep all untruths

out from my thoughts, knowing that
thou art that truth which has kindled
the light of reason in my mind.

I shall ever try to drive all evils away
from my heart and keep my love in
flower, knowing that thou hast thy seat
in the inmost shrine of my heart.

And it shall be my endeavour to
reveal thee in my actions, knowing it
is thy power gives me strength to act.

5

I ASK for a moment's indulgence to sit
by thy side. The works that I have
in hand I will finish afterwards.

Away from the sight of thy face my
heart knows no rest nor respite, and
my work becomes an endless toil in a
shoreless sea of toil.

To-day the summer has come at my
window with its sighs and murmurs;

and the bees are plying their minstrelsy at the court of the flowering grove.

Now it is time to sit quiet, face to face with thee, and to sing dedication of life in this silent and overflowing leisure.

6

PLUCK this little flower and take it, delay not! I fear lest it droop and drop into the dust.

It may not find a place in thy garland, but honour it with a touch of pain from thy hand and pluck it. I fear lest the day end before I am aware, and the time of offering go by.

Though its colour be not deep and its smell be faint, use this flower in thy service and pluck it while there is time.

7

MY song has put off her adornments.
She has no pride of dress and decora-
tion. Ornaments would mar our union ;
they would come between thee and
me ; their jingling would drown thy
whispers.

My poet's vanity dies in shame before
thy sight. O master poet, I have sat
down at thy feet. Only let me make
my life simple and straight, like a flute
of reed for thee to fill with music.

8

THE child who is decked with prince's
robes and who has jewelled chains
round his neck loses all pleasure in his
play ; his dress hampers him at every
step.

In fear that it may be frayed, or

stained with dust he keeps himself from the world, and is afraid even to move.

Mother, it is no gain, thy bondage of finery, if it keep one shut off from the healthful dust of the earth, if it rob one of the right of entrance to the great fair of common human life.

9

O FOOL, to try to carry thyself upon thy own shoulders ! O beggar, to come to beg at thy own door !

Leave all thy burdens on his hands who can bear all, and never look behind in regret.

Thy desire at once puts out the light from the lamp it touches with its breath. It is unholy—take not thy gifts through its unclean hands. Accept only what is offered by sacred love.

10

HERE is thy footstool and there rest thy feet where live the poorest, and lowliest, and lost.

When I try to bow to thee, my obeisance cannot reach down to the depth where thy feet rest among the poorest, and lowliest, and lost.

Pride can never approach to where thou walkest in the clothes of the humble among the poorest, and lowliest, and lost.

My heart can never find its way to where thou keepest company with the companionless among the poorest, the lowliest, and the lost.

11

LEAVE this chanting and singing and telling of beads! Whom dost thou worship in this lonely dark corner of a temple with doors all shut? Open thine eyes and see thy God is not before thee!

He is there where the tiller is tilling the hard ground and where the path-maker is breaking stones. He is with them in sun and in shower, and his garment is covered with dust. Put off thy holy mantle and even like him come down on the dusty soil!

Deliverance? Where is this deliver·ance to be found? Our master himself has joyfully taken upon him the bonds of creation; he is bound with us all for ever.

Come out of thy meditations and leave aside thy flowers and incense! What harm is there if thy clothes become tattered and stained? Meet him and stand by him in toil and in sweat of thy brow.

12

THE time that my journey takes is long and the way of it long.

I came out on the chariot of the first gleam of light, and pursued my voyage through the wildernesses of worlds leaving my track on many a star and planet.

It is the most distant course that comes nearest to thyself, and that training is the most intricate which leads to the utter simplicity of a tune.

The traveller has to knock at every alien door to come to his own, and one has to wander through all the outer worlds to reach the innermost shrine at the end.

My eyes strayed far and wide before I shut them and said " Here art thou ! "

The question and the cry " Oh, where ? " melt into tears of a thousand streams and deluge the world with the flood of the assurance " I am ! "

13

THE song that I came to sing remains unsung to this day.

I have spent my days in stringing and in unstringing my instrument.

The time has not come true, the words have not been rightly set; only there is the agony of wishing in my heart.

The blossom has not opened; only the wind is sighing by.

I have not seen his face, nor have I listened to his voice; only I have heard his gentle footsteps from the road before my house.

The livelong day has passed in spreading his seat on the floor; but the lamp has not been lit and 1 cannot ask him into my house.

I live in the hope of meeting with him; but this meeting is not yet.

14

My desires are many and my cry is pitiful, but ever didst thou save me by hard refusals; and this strong mercy has been wrought into my life through and through.

Day by day thou art making me worthy of the simple, great gifts that thou gavest to me unasked—this sky and the light, this body and the life and the mind—saving me from perils of overmuch desire.

There are times when I languidly linger and times when I awaken and hurry in search of my goal; but cruelly thou hidest thyself from before me.

Day by day thou art making me worthy of thy full acceptance by refusing me ever and anon, saving me from perils of weak, uncertain desire.

15

I AM here to sing thee songs. In this hall of thine I have a corner seat.

In thy world I have no work to do; my useless life can only break out in tunes without a purpose.

When the hour strikes for thy silent worship at the dark temple of midnight, command me, my master, to stand before thee to sing.

When in the morning air the golden harp is tuned, honour me, commanding my presence.

16

I HAVE had my invitation to this world's festival, and thus my life has been blessed. My eyes have seen and my ears have heard.

It was my part at this feast to play upon my instrument, and I have done all I could.

Now, I ask, has the time come at last when I may go in and see thy face and offer thee my silent salutation ?

17

I AM only waiting for love to give myself up at last into his hands. That is why it is so late and why I have been guilty of such omissions.

They come with their laws and their codes to bind me fast; but I evade them ever, for I am only waiting for love to give myself up at last into his hands.

People blame me and call me heedless; I doubt not they are right in their blame.

The market day is over and work is all done for the busy. Those who came to call me in vain have gone back in anger. I am only waiting for love to give myself up at last into his hands.

18

CLOUDS heap upon clouds and it darkens. Ah, love, why dost thou let me wait outside at the door all alone?

In the busy moments of the noontide work I am with the crowd, but on this dark lonely day it is only for thee that I hope.

If thou showest me not thy face, if thou leavest me wholly aside, I know not how I am to pass these long, rainy hours.

I keep gazing on the far-away gloom of the sky, and my heart wanders wailing with the restless wind.

19

IF thou speakest not I will fill my heart with thy silence and endure it. I will keep still and wait like the night with starry vigil and its head bent low with patience.

The morning will surely come, the darkness will vanish, and thy voice pour down in golden streams breaking through the sky.

Then thy words will take wing in songs from every one of my birds' nests, and thy melodies will break forth in flowers in all my forest groves.

20

On the day when the lotus bloomed, alas, my mind was straying, and I knew it not. My basket was empty and the flower remained unheeded.

Only now and again a sadness fell upon me, and I started up from my dream and felt a sweet trace of a strange fragrance in the south wind.

That vague sweetness made my heart ache with longing and it seemed to me

that it was the eager breath of the
summer seeking for its completion.

I knew not then that it was so near,
that it was mine, and that this perfect
sweetness had blossomed in the depth
of my own heart.

21

I MUST launch out my boat.   The
languid hours pass by on the shore—
Alas for me !

The spring has done its flowering and
taken leave.   And now with the burden
of faded futile flowers I wait and linger.

The waves have become clamorous,
and upon the bank in the shady lane the
yellow leaves flutter and fall.

What emptiness do you gaze upon !
Do you not feel a thrill passing through
the air with the notes of the far-away
song floating from the other shore ?

22

In the deep shadows of the rainy July, with secret steps, thou walkest, silent as night, eluding all watchers.

To-day the morning has closed its eyes, heedless of the insistent calls of the loud east wind, and a thick veil has been drawn over the ever-wakeful blue sky.

The woodlands have hushed their songs, and doors are all shut at every house. Thou art the solitary wayfarer in this deserted street. Oh my only friend, my best beloved, the gates are open in my house—do not pass by like a dream.

23

Art thou abroad on this stormy night on thy journey of love, my friend? The sky groans like one in despair.

I have no sleep to-night. Ever and

again I open my door and look out on
the darkness, my friend!

I can see nothing before me. I
wonder where lies thy path!

By what dim shore of the ink-black
river, by what far edge of the frowning
forest, through what mazy depth of
gloom art thou threading thy course
to come to me, my friend?

24

IF the day is done, if birds sing no
more, if the wind has flagged tired,
then draw the veil of darkness thick
upon me, even as thou hast wrapt the
earth with the coverlet of sleep and
tenderly closed the petals of the droop-
ing lotus at dusk.

From the traveller, whose sack of
provisions is empty before the voyage
is ended, whose garment is torn and
dust-laden, whose strength is exhausted,

remove shame and poverty, and renew his life like a flower under the cover of thy kindly night.

25

In the night of weariness let me give myself up to sleep without struggle, resting my trust upon thee.

Let me not force my flagging spirit into a poor preparation for thy worship.

It is thou who drawest the veil of night upon the tired eyes of the day to renew its sight in a fresher gladness of awakening.

26

He came and sat by my side but I woke not. What a cursed sleep it was, O miserable me!

He came when the night was still; he had his harp in his hands, and my dreams became resonant with its melodies.

Alas, why are my nights all thus
lost? Ah, why do I ever miss his
sight whose breath touches my sleep?

27

LIGHT, oh where is the light? Kindle
it with the burning fire of desire!

There is the lamp but never a flicker
of a flame,—is such thy fate, my heart!
Ah, death were better by far for thee!

Misery knocks at thy door, and her
message is that thy lord is wakeful, and
he calls thee to the love-tryst through
the darkness of night.

The sky is overcast with clouds and
the rain is ceaseless. I know not what
this is that stirs in me,—I know not its
meaning.

A moment's flash of lightning drags
down a deeper gloom on my sight, and
my heart gropes for the path to where
the music of the night calls me.

Light, oh where is the light! Kindle it with the burning fire of desire! It thunders and the wind rushes screaming through the void. The night is black as a black stone. Let not the hours pass by in the dark. Kindle the lamp of love with thy life.

28

OBSTINATE are the trammels, but my heart aches when I try to break them.

Freedom is all I want, but to hope for it I feel ashamed.

I am certain that priceless wealth is in thee, and that thou art my best friend, but I have not the heart to sweep away the tinsel that fills my room.

The shroud that covers me is a shroud of dust and death; I hate it, yet hug it in love.

My debts are large, my failures great,

my shame secret and heavy; yet when
I come to ask for my good, I quake in
fear lest my prayer be granted.

29

HE whom I enclose with my name is
weeping in this dungeon. I am ever
busy building this wall all around; and
as this wall goes up into the sky day
by day I lose sight of my true being in
its dark shadow.

I take pride in this great wall, and I
plaster it with dust and sand lest a least
hole should be left in this name; and
for all the care I take I lose sight of
my true being.

30

I CAME out alone on my way to my
tryst. But who is this that follows me
in the silent dark?

I move aside to avoid his presence but I escape him not.

He makes the dust rise from the earth with his swagger; he adds his loud voice to every word that I utter.

He is my own little self, my lord, he knows no shame; but I am ashamed to come to thy door in his company.

31

"Prisoner, tell me, who was it that bound you?"

"It was my master," said the prisoner. "I thought I could outdo everybody in the world in wealth and power, and I amassed in my own treasure-house the money due to my king. When sleep overcame me I lay upon the bed that was for my lord, and on waking up I found I was a prisoner in my own treasure-house."

"Prisoner, tell me, who was it that wrought this unbreakable chain?"

"It was I," said the prisoner, "who forged this chain very carefully. I thought my invincible power would hold the world captive leaving me in a freedom undisturbed. Thus night and day I worked at the chain with huge fires and cruel hard strokes. When at last the work was done and the links were complete and unbreakable, I found that it held me in its grip."

32

By all means they try to hold me secure who love me in this world. But it is otherwise with thy love which is greater than theirs, and thou keepest me free.

Lest I forget them they never venture to leave me alone. But day passes by after day and thou art not seen.

If I call not thee in my prayers, if I keep not thee in my heart, thy love for me still waits for my love.

33

WHEN it was day they came into my house and said, "We shall only take the smallest room here."

They said, "We shall help you in the worship of your God and humbly accept only our own share of his grace"; and then they took their seat in a corner and they sat quiet and meek.

But in the darkness of night I find they break into my sacred shrine, strong and turbulent, and snatch with unholy greed the offerings from God's altar.

34

LET only that little be left of me whereby I may name thee my all.

Let only that little be left of my will whereby I may feel thee on every side, and come to thee in everything, and offer to thee my love every moment.

Let only that little be left of me whereby I may never hide thee.

Let only that little of my fetters be left whereby I am bound with thy will, and thy purpose is carried out in my life—and that is the fetter of thy love.

35

WHERE the mind is without fear and the head is held high;

Where knowledge is free;

Where the world has not been broken up into fragments by narrow domestic walls;

Where words come out from the depth of truth;

Where tireless striving stretches its arms towards perfection:

Where the clear stream of reason has not lost its way into the dreary desert sand of dead habit ;

Where the mind is led forward by thee into ever-widening thought and action—

Into that heaven of freedom, my Father, let my country awake.

36

THIS is my prayer to thee, my lord— strike, strike at the root of penury in my heart.

Give me the strength lightly to bear my joys and sorrows.

Give me the strength to make my love fruitful in service.

Give me the strength never to disown the poor or bend my knees before insolent might.

Give me the strength to raise my mind high above daily trifles.

And give me the strength to surrender my strength to thy will with love.

37

I THOUGHT that my voyage had come to its end at the last limit of my power, —that the path before me was closed, that provisions were exhausted and the time come to take shelter in a silent obscurity.

But I find that thy will knows no end in me. And when old words die out on the tongue, new melodies break forth from the heart; and where the old tracks are lost, new country is revealed with its wonders.

38

THAT I want thee, only thee—let my heart repeat without end. All desires that distract me, day and night, are false and empty to the core.

As the night keeps hidden in its gloom the petition for light, even thus in the depth of my unconsciousness rings the cry—I want thee, only thee.

As the storm still seeks its end in peace when it strikes against peace with all its might, even thus my rebellion strikes against thy love and still its cry is—I want thee, only thee.

39

WHEN the heart is hard and parched up, come upon me with a shower of mercy.

When grace is lost from life, come with a burst of song.

When tumultuous work raises its din on all sides shutting me out from beyond, come to me, my lord of silence, with thy peace and rest.

When my beggarly heart sits crouched, shut up in a corner, break open the door,

my king, and come with the ceremony
of a king.

When desire blinds the mind with
delusion and dust, O thou holy one,
thou wakeful, come with thy light and
thy thunder.

40

THE rain has held back for days and
days, my God, in my arid heart. The
horizon is fiercely naked—not the thin-
nest cover of a soft cloud, not the
vaguest hint of a distant cool shower.

Send thy angry storm, dark with
death, if it is thy wish, and with lashes
of lightning startle the sky from end to
end.

But call back, my lord, call back
this pervading silent heat, still and keen
and cruel, burning the heart with dire
despair.

Let the cloud of grace bend low from

above like the tearful look of the mother
on the day of the father's wrath.

41

WHERE dost thou stand behind them
all, my lover, hiding thyself in the
shadows? They push thee and pass
thee by on the dusty road, taking thee
for naught. I wait here weary hours
spreading my offerings for thee, while
passers by come and take my flowers,
one by one, and my basket is nearly
empty.

The morning time is past, and the
noon. In the shade of evening my
eyes are drowsy with sleep. Men going
home glance at me and smile and fill
me with shame. I sit like a beggar
maid, drawing my skirt over my face,
and when they ask me, what it is I
want, I drop my eyes and answer them
not.

Oh, how, indeed, could I tell them that for thee I wait, and that thou hast promised to come. How could I utter for shame that I keep for my dowry this poverty. Ah, I hug this pride in the secret of my heart.

I sit on the grass and gaze upon the sky and dream of the sudden splendour of thy coming—all the lights ablaze, golden pennons flying over thy car, and they at the roadside standing agape, when they see thee come down from thy seat to raise me from the dust, and set at thy side this ragged beggar girl a-tremble with shame and pride, like a creeper in a summer breeze.

But time glides on and still no sound of the wheels of thy chariot. Many a procession passes by with noise and shouts and glamour of glory. Is it only thou who wouldst stand in the shadow silent and behind them all ? And only I

who would wait and weep and wear out
my heart in vain longing?

42

EARLY in the day it was whispered that
we should sail in a boat, only thou and
I, and never a soul in the world would
know of this our pilgrimage to no
country and to no end.

In that shoreless ocean, at thy silently
listening smile my songs would swell
in melodies, free as waves, free from all
bondage of words.

Is the time not come yet? Are there
works still to do? Lo, the evening
has come down upon the shore and in
the fading light the seabirds come
flying to their nests.

Who knows when the chains will be
off, and the boat, like the last glimmer
of sunset, vanish into the night?

43

THE day was when I did not keep myself in readiness for thee; and entering my heart unbidden even as one of the common crowd, unknown to me, my king, thou didst press the signet of eternity upon many a fleeting moment of my life.

And to-day when by chance I light upon them and see thy signature, I find they have lain scattered in the dust mixed with the memory of joys and sorrows of my trivial days forgotten.

Thou didst not turn in contempt from my childish play among dust, and the steps that I heard in my playroom are the same that are echoing from star to star.

44

THIS is my delight, thus to wait and watch at the wayside where shadow chases light and the rain comes in the wake of the summer.

Messengers, with tidings from unknown skies, greet me and speed along the road. My heart is glad within, and the breath of the passing breeze is sweet.

From dawn till dusk I sit here before my door, and I know that of a sudden the happy moment will arrive when I shall see.

In the meanwhile I smile and I sing all alone. In the meanwhile the air is filling with the perfume of promise.

45

HAVE you not heard his silent steps? He comes, comes, ever comes.

Every moment and every age, every day and every night he comes, comes, ever comes.

Many a song have I sung in many a mood of mind, but all their notes have always proclaimed, "He comes, comes, ever comes."

In the fragrant days of sunny April through the forest path he comes, comes, ever comes.

In the rainy gloom of July nights on the thundering chariot of clouds he comes, comes, ever comes.

In sorrow after sorrow it is his steps that press upon my heart, and it is the golden touch of his feet that makes my joy to shine.

46

I KNOW not from what distant time thou art ever coming nearer to meet me.   Thy sun and stars can never keep thee hidden from me for aye.

In many a morning and eve thy footsteps have been heard and thy messenger has come within my heart and called me in secret.

I know not why to-day my life is all astir, and a feeling of tremulous joy is passing through my heart.

It is as if the time were come to wind up my work, and I feel in the air a faint smell of thy sweet presence.

47

THE night is nearly spent waiting for him in vain.   I fear lest in the morning he suddenly come to my door when I have fallen asleep wearied out.   Oh friends, leave the way open to him— forbid him not.

If the sound of his steps does not wake me, do not try to rouse me, I pray. I wish not to be called from my sleep by the clamorous choir of birds, by the riot of wind at the festival of morning light. Let me sleep undisturbed even if my lord comes of a sudden to my door.

Ah, my sleep, precious sleep, which only waits for his touch to vanish. Ah, my closed eyes that would open their lids only to the light of his smile when he stands before me like a dream emerging from darkness of sleep.

Let him appear before my sight as the first of all lights and all forms. The first thrill of joy to my awakened soul let it come from his glance. And let my return to myself be immediate return to him.

48

THE morning sea of silence broke into ripples of bird songs ; and the flowers

were all merry by the roadside ; and
the wealth of gold was scattered
through the rift of the clouds while
we busily went on our way and paid no
heed.

We sang no glad songs nor played ;
we went not to the village for barter ;
we spoke not a word nor smiled ;
we lingered not on the way. We
quickened our pace more and more as
the time sped by.

The sun rose to the mid sky and
doves cooed in the shade. Withered
leaves danced and whirled in the hot
air of noon. The shepherd boy drowsed
and dreamed in the shadow of the
banyan tree, and I laid myself down
by the water and stretched my tired
limbs on the grass.

My companions laughed at me in
scorn ; they held their heads high and
hurried on ; they never looked back nor
rested ; they vanished in the distant

blue haze. They crossed many meadows and hills, and passed through strange, far - away countries. All honour to you, heroic host of the interminable path! Mockery and reproach pricked me to rise, but found no response in me. I gave myself up for lost in the depth of a glad humiliation — in the shadow of a dim delight.

The repose of the sun-embroidered green gloom slowly spread over my heart. I forgot for what I had travelled, and I surrendered my mind without struggle to the maze of shadows and songs.

At last, when I woke from my slumber and opened my eyes, I saw thee standing by me, flooding my sleep with thy smile. How I had feared that the path was long and wearisome, and the struggle to reach thee was hard!

49

You came down from your throne and stood at my cottage door.

I was singing all alone in a corner, and the melody caught your ear. You came down and stood at my cottage door.

Masters are many in your hall, and songs are sung there at all hours. But the simple carol of this novice struck at your love. One plaintive little strain mingled with the great music of the world, and with a flower for a prize you came down and stopped at my cottage door.

50

I HAD gone a-begging from door to door in the village path, when thy golden chariot appeared in the distance like a gorgeous dream and I wondered who was this King of all kings!

My hopes rose high and methought my evil days were at an end, and I stood waiting for alms to be given unasked and for wealth scattered on all sides in the dust.

The chariot stopped where I stood. Thy glance fell on me and thou camest down with a smile. I felt that the luck of my life had come at last. Then of a sudden thou didst hold out thy right hand and say "What hast thou to give to me?"

Ah, what a kingly jest was it to open thy palm to a beggar to beg! I was confused and stood undecided, and then from my wallet I slowly took out the least little grain of corn and gave it to thee.

But how great my surprise when at the day's end I emptied my bag on the floor to find a least little grain of gold among the poor heap. I bitterly wept and wished that I had had the heart to give thee my all.

51

THE night darkened. Our day's works
had been done. We thought that
the last guest had arrived for the night
and the doors in the village were all
shut. Only some said, The king was
to come. We laughed and said "No,
it cannot be!"

It seemed there were knocks at the
door and we said it was nothing but
the wind. We put out the lamps and
lay down to sleep. Only some said,
"It is the messenger!" We laughed
and said "No, it must be the wind!"

There came a sound in the dead of
the night. We sleepily thought it was
the distant thunder. The earth shook,
the walls rocked, and it troubled us in
our sleep. Only some said, it was the
sound of wheels. We said in a drowsy
murmur, "No, it must be the rumbling
of clouds!"

The night was still dark when the drum sounded. The voice came " Wake up ! delay not ! " We pressed our hands on our hearts and shuddered with fear. Some said, " Lo, there is the king's flag ! " We stood up on our feet and cried " There is no time for delay ! "

The king has come—but where are lights, where are wreaths ? Where is the throne to seat him ? Oh, shame, Oh utter shame ! Where is the hall, the decorations ? Some one has said, " Vain is this cry ! Greet him with empty hands, lead him into thy rooms all bare ! "

Open the doors, let the conch-shells be sounded ! In the depth of the night has come the king of our dark, dreary house. The thunder roars in the sky. The darkness shudders with lightning. Bring out thy tattered piece of mat and spread it in the courtyard. With the storm has come

of a sudden our king of the fearful
night.

52

1 THOUGHT I should ask of thee—but
I dared not — the rose wreath thou
hadst on thy neck. Thus I waited
for the morning, when thou didst
depart, to find a few fragments on the
bed. And like a beggar I searched
in the dawn only for a stray petal or
two.

Ah me, what is it I find? What
token left of thy love? It is no
flower, no spices, no vase of perfumed
water. It is thy mighty sword,
flashing as a flame, heavy as a bolt
of thunder. The young light of
morning comes through the window
and spreads itself upon thy bed. The
morning bird twitters and asks,
" Woman, what hast thou got?" No,

it is no flower, nor spices, nor vase of perfumed water — it is thy dreadful sword.

I sit and muse in wonder, what gift is this of thine. I can find no place where to hide it. I am ashamed to wear it, frail as I am, and it hurts me when I press it to my bosom. Yet shall I bear in my heart this honour of the burden of pain, this gift of thine.

From now there shall be no fear left for me in this world, and thou shalt be victorious in all my strife. Thou hast left death for my companion and I shall crown him with my life. Thy sword is with me to cut asunder my bonds, and there shall be no fear left for me in the world.

From now I leave off all petty decorations. Lord of my heart, no more shall there be for me waiting and weeping in corners, no more coyness and sweetness of demeanour. Thou

hast given me thy sword for adornment.
No more doll's decorations for me !

53

BEAUTIFUL is thy wristlet, decked
with stars and cunningly wrought in
myriad - coloured jewels. But more
beautiful to me thy sword with its
curve of lightning like the outspread
wings of the divine bird of Vishnu,
perfectly poised in the angry red light
of the sunset.

It quivers like the one last response
of life in ecstasy of pain at the final
stroke of death ; it shines like the pure
flame of being burning up earthly sense
with one fierce flash.

Beautiful is thy wristlet, decked
with starry gems ; but thy sword, O
lord of thunder, is wrought with
uttermost beauty, terrible to behold
or to think of.

54

I ASKED nothing from thee; I uttered not my name to thine ear. When thou took'st thy leave I stood silent. I was alone by the well where the shadow of the tree fell aslant, and the women had gone home with their brown earthen pitchers full to the brim. They called me and shouted, "Come with us, the morning is wearing on to noon." But I languidly lingered awhile lost in the midst of vague musings.

I heard not thy steps as thou camest. Thine eyes were sad when they fell on me; thy voice was tired as thou spokest low — "Ah, I am a thirsty traveller." I started up from my day-dreams and poured water from my jar on thy joined palms. The leaves rustled overhead; the cuckoo sang from the unseen dark, and perfume of *babla* flowers came from the bend of the road.

I stood speechless with shame when my name thou didst ask. Indeed, what had I done for thee to keep me in remembrance? But the memory that I could give water to thee to allay thy thirst will cling to my heart and enfold it in sweetness. The morning hour is late, the bird sings in weary notes, *neem* leaves rustle overhead and I sit and think and think.

55

LANGUOR is upon your heart and the slumber is still on your eyes.

Has not the word come to you that the flower is reigning in splendour among thorns? Wake, oh awaken! Let not the time pass in vain!

At the end of the stony path, in the country of virgin solitude my friend is sitting all alone. Deceive him not. Wake, oh awaken!

What if the sky pants and trembles with the heat of the midday sun—what if the burning sand spreads its mantle of thirst—

Is there no joy in the deep of your heart? At every footfall of yours, will not the harp of the road break out in sweet music of pain?

56

Thus it is that thy joy in me is so full. Thus it is that thou hast come down to me. O thou lord of all heavens, where would be thy love if I were not?

Thou hast taken me as thy partner of all this wealth. In my heart is the endless play of thy delight. In my life thy will is ever taking shape.

And for this, thou who art the King

of kings hast decked thyself in beauty
to captivate my heart. And for this
thy love loses itself in the love of thy
lover, and there art thou seen in the
perfect union of two.

57

Light, my light, the world-filling light,
the eye-kissing light, heart-sweetening
light !

Ah, the light dances, my darling, at
the centre of my life ; the light strikes,
my darling, the chords of my love ; the
sky opens, the wind runs wild, laughter
passes over the earth.

The butterflies spread their sails on
the sea of light. Lilies and jasmines
surge up on the crest of the waves of
light.

The light is shattered into gold on
every cloud, my darling, and it scatters
gems in profusion.

Mirth spreads from leaf to leaf, my darling, and gladness without measure. The heaven's river has drowned its banks and the flood of joy is abroad.

58

LET all the strains of joy mingle in my last song—the joy that makes the earth flow over in the riotous excess of the grass, the joy that sets the twin brothers, life and death, dancing over the wide world, the joy that sweeps in with the tempest, shaking and waking all life with laughter, the joy that sits still with its tears on the open red lotus of pain, and the joy that throws everything it has upon the dust, and knows not a word.

59

YES, I know, this is nothing but thy love, O beloved of my heart—this golden light that dances upon the leaves, these idle clouds sailing across the sky, this passing breeze leaving its coolness upon my forehead.

The morning light has flooded my eyes—this is thy message to my heart. Thy face is bent from above, thy eyes look down on my eyes, and my heart has touched thy feet.

60

On the seashore of endless worlds children meet. The infinite sky is motionless overhead and the restless water is boisterous. On the seashore of endless worlds the children meet with shouts and dances.

They build their houses with sand and they play with empty shells. With withered leaves they weave their boats and smilingly float them on the vast

deep. Children have their play on the
seashore of worlds.

They know not how to swim, they
know not how to cast nets. Pearl
fishers dive for pearls, merchants sail in
their ships, while children gather pebbles
and scatter them again. They seek not
for hidden treasures, they know not how
to cast nets.

The sea surges up with laughter and
pale gleams the smile of the sea beach.
Death-dealing waves sing meaningless
ballads to the children, even like a
mother while rocking her baby's cradle.
The sea plays with children, and pale
gleams the smile of the sea beach.

On the seashore of endless worlds
children meet. Tempest roams in the
pathless sky, ships get wrecked in the
trackless water, death is abroad and
children play. On the seashore of end-
less worlds is the great meeting of
children.

61

THE sleep that flits on baby's eyes—does anybody know from where it comes? Yes, there is a rumour that it has its dwelling where, in the fairy village among shadows of the forest dimly lit with glow-worms, there hang two timid buds of enchantment. From there it comes to kiss baby's eyes.

The smile that flickers on baby's lips when he sleeps—does anybody know where it was born? Yes, there is a rumour that a young pale beam of a crescent moon touched the edge of a vanishing autumn cloud, and there the smile was first born in the dream of a dew-washed morning — the smile that flickers on baby's lips when he sleeps.

The sweet, soft freshness that blooms on baby's limbs—does anybody know where it was hidden so long? Yes, when the mother was a young girl it

lay pervading her heart in tender and
silent mystery of love—the sweet, soft
freshness that has bloomed on baby's
limbs.

62

WHEN I bring to you coloured toys,
my child, I understand why there is
such a play of colours on clouds, on
water, and why flowers are painted in
tints—when I give coloured toys to
you, my child.

When I sing to make you dance I
truly know why there is music in leaves,
and why waves send their chorus of
voices to the heart of the listening
earth—when I sing to make you dance.

When I bring sweet things to your
greedy hands I know why there is
honey in the cup of the flower and why
fruits are secretly filled with sweet juice
—when I bring sweet things to your
greedy hands.

F

When I kiss your face to make you smile, my darling, I surely understand what the pleasure is that streams from the sky in morning light, and what delight that is which the summer breeze brings to my body—when I kiss you to make you smile.

63

THOU hast made me known to friends whom I knew not. Thou hast given me seats in homes not my own. Thou hast brought the distant near and made a brother of the stranger.

I am uneasy at heart when I have to leave my accustomed shelter; I forget that there abides the old in the new, and that there also thou abidest.

Through birth and death, in this world or in others, wherever thou leadest me it is thou, the same, the one companion of my endless life who ever linkest my heart with bonds of joy to the unfamiliar.

When one knows thee, then alien there is none, then no door is shut. Oh, grant me my prayer that I may never lose the bliss of the touch of the one in the play of the many.

64

On the slope of the desolate river among tall grasses I asked her, " Maiden, where do you go shading your lamp with your mantle? My house is all dark and lonesome—lend me your light!" She raised her dark eyes for a moment and looked at my face through the dusk. "I have come to the river," she said, "to float my lamp on the stream when the daylight wanes in the west." I stood alone among tall grasses and watched the timid flame of her lamp uselessly drifting in the tide.

In the silence of gathering night I asked her, "Maiden, your lights are all lit—then where do you go with your lamp? My house is all dark and lonesome,—lend me your light." She raised her dark eyes on my face and stood for a moment doubtful. "I have come," she said at last, "to dedicate my lamp to the sky." I stood and watched her light uselessly burning in the void.

In the moonless gloom of midnight I asked her, "Maiden, what is your quest holding the lamp near your heart? My house is all dark and lonesome,—lend me your light." She stopped for a minute and thought and gazed at my face in the dark. "I have brought my light," she said, "to join the carnival of lamps." I stood and watched her little lamp uselessly lost among lights.

65

WHAT divine drink wouldst thou have, my God, from this overflowing cup of my life?

My poet, is it thy delight to see thy creation through my eyes and to stand at the portals of my ears silently to listen to thine own eternal harmony?

Thy world is weaving words in my mind and thy joy is adding music to them. Thou givest thyself to me in love and then feelest thine own entire sweetness in me.

66

SHE who ever had remained in the depth of my being, in the twilight of gleams and of glimpses; she who never opened her veils in the morning light, will be my last gift to thee, my God, folded in my final song.

Words have wooed yet failed to win her ; persuasion has stretched to her its eager arms in vain.

I have roamed from country to country keeping her in the core of my heart, and around her have risen and fallen the growth and decay of my life.

Over my thoughts and actions, my slumbers and dreams, she reigned yet dwelled alone and apart.

Many a man knocked at my door and asked for her and turned away in despair.

There was none in the world who ever saw her face to face, and she remained in her loneliness waiting for thy recognition.

67

THOU art the sky and thou art the nest as well.

O thou beautiful, there in the nest it

is thy love that encloses the soul with colours and sounds and odours.

There comes the morning with the golden basket in her right hand bearing the wreath of beauty, silently to crown the earth.

And there comes the evening over the lonely meadows deserted by herds, through trackless paths, carrying cool draughts of peace in her golden pitcher from the western ocean of rest.

But there, where spreads the infinite sky for the soul to take her flight in, reigns the stainless white radiance. There is no day nor night, nor form nor colour, and never, never a word.

68

THY sunbeam comes upon this earth of mine with arms outstretched and stands at my door the livelong day to carry back to thy feet clouds made of my tears and sighs and songs.

With fond delight thou wrappest about thy starry breast that mantle of misty cloud, turning it into numberless shapes and folds and colouring it with hues everchanging.

It is so light and so fleeting, tender and tearful and dark, that is why thou lovest it, O thou spotless and serene. And that is why it may cover thy awful white light with its pathetic shadows.

69

THE same stream of life that runs through my veins night and day runs through the world and dances in rhythmic measures.

It is the same life that shoots in joy through the dust of the earth in numberless blades of grass and breaks into tumultuous waves of leaves and flowers.

It is the same life that is rocked in the ocean-cradle of birth and of death, in ebb and in flow.

I feel my limbs are made glorious by the touch of this world of life. And my pride is from the life-throb of ages dancing in my blood this moment.

70

Is it beyond thee to be glad with the gladness of this rhythm ? to be tossed and lost and broken in the whirl of this fearful joy ?

All things rush on, they stop not, they look not behind, no power can hold them back, they rush on.

Keeping steps with that restless, rapid music, seasons come dancing and pass away — colours, tunes, and perfumes pour in endless cascades in the abound·

ing joy that scatters and gives up and dies every moment.

71

THAT I should make much of myself and turn it on all sides, thus casting coloured shadows on thy radiance — such is thy *maya*.

Thou settest a barrier in thine own being and then callest thy severed self in myriad notes. This thy self-separation has taken body in me.

The poignant song is echoed through all the sky in many-coloured tears and smiles, alarms and hopes; waves rise up and sink again, dreams break and form. In me is thy own defeat of self.

This screen that thou hast raised is painted with innumerable figures with the brush of the night and the day. Behind it thy seat is woven in wondrous mysteries of curves, casting away all barren lines of straightness.

The great pageant of thee and me has overspread the sky. With the tune of thee and me all the air is vibrant, and all ages pass with the hiding and seeking of thee and me.

72

HE it is, the innermost one, who awakens my being with his deep hidden touches.

He it is who puts his enchantment upon these eyes and joyfully plays on the chords of my heart in varied cadence of pleasure and pain.

He it is who weaves the web of this *maya* in evanescent hues of gold and silver, blue and green, and lets peep out through the folds his feet, at whose touch I forget myself.

Days come and ages pass, and it is ever he who moves my heart in many a

name, in many a guise, in many a
rapture of joy and of sorrow.

73

DELIVERANCE is not for me in renuncia-
tion. I feel the embrace of freedom in
a thousand bonds of delight.

Thou ever pourest for me the fresh
draught of thy wine of various colours
and fragrance, filling this earthen vessel
to the brim.

My world will light its hundred
different lamps with thy flame and
place them before the altar of thy
temple.

No, I will never shut the doors of
my senses. The delights of sight and
hearing and touch will bear thy delight.

Yes, all my illusions will burn into
illumination of joy, and all my desires
ripen into fruits of love.

74

THE day is no more, the shadow is upon the earth. It is time that I go to the stream to fill my pitcher.

The evening air is eager with the sad music of the water. Ah, it calls me out into the dusk. In the lonely lane there is no passer by, the wind is up, the ripples are rampant in the river.

I know not if I shall come back home. I know not whom I shall chance to meet. There at the fording in the little boat the unknown man plays upon his lute.

75

THY gifts to us mortals fulfil all our needs and yet run back to thee undiminished.

The river has its everyday work to do and hastens through fields and hamlets ; yet its incessant stream winds towards the washing of thy feet.

The flower sweetens the air with its perfume ; yet its last service is to offer itself to thee.

Thy worship does not impoverish the world.

From the words of the poet men take what meanings please them ; yet their last meaning points to thee.

76

DAY after day, O lord of my life, shall I stand before thee face to face. With folded hands, O lord of all worlds, shall I stand before thee face to face.

Under thy great sky in solitude and silence, with humble heart shall I stand before thee face to face.

In this laborious world of thine, tumultuous with toil and with struggle, among hurrying crowds shall I stand before thee face to face.

And when my work shall be done in this world, O King of kings, alone and speechless shall I stand before thee face to face.

77

I know thee as my God and stand apart—I do not know thee as my own and come closer. I know thee as my father and bow before thy feet—I do not grasp thy hand as my friend's.

I stand not where thou comest down and ownest thyself as mine, there to clasp thee to my heart and take thee as my comrade.

Thou art the Brother amongst my brothers, but I heed them not, I divide not my earnings with them, thus sharing my all with thee.

In pleasure and in pain I stand not

by the side of men, and thus stand
by thee. I shrink to give up my
life, and thus do not plunge into the
great waters of life.

78

WHEN the creation was new and all
the stars shone in their first splendour,
the gods held their assembly in the sky
and sang "Oh, the picture of perfec-
tion ! the joy unalloyed !"

But one cried of a sudden—" It seems
that somewhere there is a break in the
chain of light and one of the stars has
been lost."

The golden string of their harp
snapped, their song stopped, and they
cried in dismay—"Yes, that lost star
was the best, she was the glory of all
heavens !"

From that day the search is un-
ceasing for her, and the cry goes on

from one to the other that in her the
world has lost its one joy!

Only in the deepest silence of night
the stars smile and whisper among
themselves — "Vain is this seeking!
Unbroken perfection is over all!"

79

IF it is not my portion to meet thee in
this my life then let me ever feel that
I have missed thy sight — let me not
forget for a moment, let me carry the
pangs of this sorrow in my dreams and
in my wakeful hours.

As my days pass in the crowded
market of this world and my hands
grow full with the daily profits, let me
ever feel that I have gained nothing—
let me not forget for a moment, let me
carry the pangs of this sorrow in my
dreams and in my wakeful hours.

When I sit by the roadside, tired

and panting, when I spread my bed low
in the dust, let me ever feel that the
long journey is still before me—let me
not forget for a moment, let me carry
the pangs of this sorrow in my dreams
and in my wakeful hours.

When my rooms have been decked
out and the flutes sound and the laughter
there is loud, let me ever feel that I
have not invited thee to my house—
let me not forget for a moment, let me
carry the pangs of this sorrow in my
dreams and in my wakeful hours.

80

I AM like a remnant of a cloud of
autumn uselessly roaming in the sky, O
my sun ever-glorious! Thy touch has
not yet melted my vapour, making me
one with thy light, and thus I count
months and years separated from thee.

If this be thy wish and if this be thy

play, then take this fleeting emptiness of mine, paint it with colours, gild it with gold, float it on the wanton wind and spread it in varied wonders.

And again when it shall be thy wish to end this play at night, I shall melt and vanish away in the dark, or it may be in a smile of the white morning, in a coolness of purity transparent.

81

On many an idle day have I grieved over lost time. But it is never lost, my lord. Thou hast taken every moment of my life in thine own hands.

Hidden in the heart of things thou art nourishing seeds into sprouts, buds into blossoms, and ripening flowers into fruitfulness.

I was tired and sleeping on my idle bed and imagined all work had ceased.

In the morning I woke up and found
my garden full with wonders of flowers.

82

TIME is endless in thy hands, my lord.
There is none to count thy minutes.

Days and nights pass and ages bloom
and fade like flowers. Thou knowest
how to wait.

Thy centuries follow each other
perfecting a small wild flower.

We have no time to lose, and having
no time we must scramble for our
chances. We are too poor to be late.

And thus it is that time goes by
while I give it to every querulous man
who claims it, and thine altar is empty
of all offerings to the last.

At the end of the day I hasten in
fear lest thy gate be shut; but I find
that yet there is time.

83

MOTHER, I shall weave a chain of pearls for thy neck with my tears of sorrow.

The stars have wrought their anklets of light to deck thy feet, but mine will hang upon thy breast.

Wealth and fame come from thee and it is for thee to give or to withhold them. But this my sorrow is absolutely mine own, and when I bring it to thee as my offering thou rewardest me with thy grace.

84

IT is the pang of separation that spreads throughout the world and gives birth to shapes innumerable in the infinite sky.

It is this sorrow of separation that gazes in silence all night from star to star and becomes lyric among rustling leaves in rainy darkness of July.

It is this overspreading pain that deepens into loves and desires, into sufferings and joys in human homes; and this it is that ever melts and flows in songs through my poet's heart.

85

WHEN the warriors came out first from their master's hall, where had they hid their power? Where were their armour and their arms?

They looked poor and helpless, and the arrows were showered upon them on the day they came out from their master's hall.

When the warriors marched back again to their master's hall where did they hide their power?

They had dropped the sword and dropped the bow and the arrow; peace was on their foreheads, and they had left the fruits of their life behind them on the day they marched back again to their master's hall.

86

DEATH, thy servant, is at my door. He has crossed the unknown sea and brought thy call to my home.

The night is dark and my heart is fearful—yet I will take up the lamp, open my gates and bow to him my welcome. It is thy messenger who stands at my door.

I will worship him with folded hands, and with tears. I will worship him placing at his feet the treasure of my heart.

He will go back with his errand done, leaving a dark shadow on my morning; and in my desolate home only my forlorn self will remain as my last offering to thee.

87

IN desperate hope I go and search for her in all the corners of my room; I find her not.

My house is small and what once has gone from it can never be regained.

But infinite is thy mansion, my lord, and seeking her I have come to thy door.

I stand under the golden canopy of thine evening sky and I lift my eager eyes to thy face.

I have come to the brink of eternity from which nothing can vanish — no hope, no happiness, no vision of a face seen through tears.

Oh, dip my emptied life into that ocean, plunge it into the deepest fullness. Let me for once feel that lost sweet touch in the allness of the universe.

88

Deity of the ruined temple! The broken strings of *Vina* sing no more your praise. The bells in the evening proclaim not your time of worship. The air is still and silent about you.

In your desolate dwelling comes the vagrant spring breeze. It brings the tidings of flowers—the flowers that for your worship are offered no more.

Your worshipper of old wanders ever longing for favour still refused. In the eventide, when fires and shadows mingle with the gloom of dust, he wearily comes back to the ruined temple with hunger in his heart.

Many a festival day comes to you in silence, deity of the ruined temple. Many a night of worship goes away with lamp unlit.

Many new images are built by masters of cunning art and carried to

the holy stream of oblivion when their
time is come.

Only the deity of the ruined temple
remains unworshipped in deathless
neglect.

89

No more noisy, loud words from me—
such is my master's will. Henceforth
I deal in whispers. The speech of my
heart will be carried on in murmurings
of a song.

Men hasten to the King's market.
All the buyers and sellers are there.
But I have my untimely leave in the
middle of the day, in the thick of work.

Let then the flowers come out in my
garden, though it is not their time;
and let the midday bees strike up their
lazy hum.

Full many an hour have I spent in
the strife of the good and the evil, but
now it is the pleasure of my playmate

of the empty days to draw my heart on
to him; and I know not why is this
sudden call to what useless incon-
sequence!

90

ON the day when death will knock at
thy door what wilt thou offer to him?

Oh, I will set before my guest the
full vessel of my life—I will never let
him go with empty hands.

All the sweet vintage of all my
autumn days and summer nights, all
the earnings and gleanings of my busy
life will I place before him at the close
of my days when death will knock at
my door.

91

O THOU the last fulfilment of life, Death,
my death, come and whisper to me!

Day after day have I kept watch for

thee; for thee have I borne the joys and pangs of life.

All that I am, that I have, that I hope and all my love have ever flowed towards thee in depth of secrecy. One final glance from thine eyes and my life will be ever thine own.

The flowers have been woven and the garland is ready for the bridegroom. After the wedding the bride shall leave her home and meet her lord alone in the solitude of night.

92

I KNOW that the day will come when my sight of this earth shall be lost, and life will take its leave in silence, drawing the last curtain over my eyes.

Yet stars will watch at night, and morning rise as before, and hours heave like sea waves casting up pleasures and pains.

When I think of this end of my
moments, the barrier of the moments
breaks and I see by the light of death
thy world with its careless treasures.
Rare is its lowliest seat, rare is its
meanest of lives.

Things that I longed for in vain and
things that I got—let them pass. Let
me but truly possess the things that I
ever spurned and overlooked.

93

I HAVE got my leave. Bid me farewell,
my brothers! I bow to you all and
take my departure.

Here I give back the keys of my
door—and I give up all claims to my
house. I only ask for last kind words
from you.

We were neighbours for long, but I
received more than I could give. Now
the day has dawned and the lamp

that lit my dark corner is out. A summons has come and I am ready for my journey.

94

At this time of my parting, wish me good luck, my friends! The sky is flushed with the dawn and my path lies beautiful.

Ask not what I have with me to take there. I start on my journey with empty hands and expectant heart.

I shall put on my wedding garland. Mine is not the red-brown dress of the traveller, and though there are dangers on the way I have no fear in my mind.

The evening star will come out when my voyage is done and the plaintive notes of the twilight melodies be struck up from the King's gateway.

95

I WAS not aware of the moment when I first crossed the threshold of this life.

What was the power that made me open out into this vast mystery like a bud in the forest at midnight!

When in the morning I looked upon the light I felt in a moment that I was no stranger in this world, that the inscrutable without name and form had taken me in its arms in the form of my own mother.

Even so, in death the same unknown will appear as ever known to me. And because I love this life, I know I shall love death as well.

The child cries out when from the right breast the mother takes it away, in the very next moment to find in the left one its consolation.

96

WHEN I go from hence let this be my parting word, that what I have seen is unsurpassable.

I have tasted of the hidden honey of this lotus that expands on the ocean of light, and thus am I blessed—let this be my parting word.

In this playhouse of infinite forms I have had my play and here have I caught sight of him that is formless.

My whole body and my limbs have thrilled with his touch who is beyond touch ; and if the end comes here, let it come—let this be my parting word.

97

WHEN my play was with thee I never questioned who thou wert. I knew nor shyness nor fear, my life was boisterous.

In the early morning thou wouldst

call me from my sleep like my own comrade and lead me running from glade to glade.

On those days I never cared to know the meaning of songs thou sangest to me. Only my voice took up the tunes, and my heart danced in their cadence.

Now, when the playtime is over, what is this sudden sight that is come upon me? The world with eyes bent upon thy feet stands in awe with all its silent stars.

98

I will deck thee with trophies, garlands of my defeat. It is never in my power to escape unconquered.

I surely know my pride will go to the wall, my life will burst its bonds in exceeding pain, and my empty heart will sob out in music like a hollow reed, and the stone will melt in tears.

I surely know the hundred petals of

H

a lotus will not remain closed for ever and the secret recess of its honey will be bared.

From the blue sky an eye shall gaze upon me and summon me in silence. Nothing will be left for me, nothing whatever, and utter death shall I receive at thy feet.

99

WHEN I give up the helm I know that the time has come for thee to take it. What there is to do will be instantly done. Vain is this struggle.

Then take away your hands and silently put up with your defeat, my heart, and think it your good fortune to sit perfectly still where you are placed.

These my lamps are blown out at every little puff of wind, and trying to light them I forget all else again and again.

But I shall be wise this time and wait in the dark, spreading my mat on the floor; and whenever it is thy pleasure, my lord, come silently and take thy seat here.

100

I DIVE down into the depth of the ocean of forms, hoping to gain the perfect pearl of the formless.

No more sailing from harbour to harbour with this my weather-beaten boat. The days are long passed when my sport was to be tossed on waves.

And now I am eager to die into the deathless.

Into the audience hall by the fathomless abyss where swells up the music of toneless strings I shall take this harp of my life.

I shall tune it to the notes of for ever, and, when it has sobbed out its last utterance, lay down my silent harp at the feet of the silent.

101

EVER in my life have I sought thee with my songs. It was they who led me from door to door, and with them have I felt about me, searching and touching my world.

It was my songs that taught me all the lessons I ever learnt; they showed me secret paths, they brought before my sight many a star on the horizon of my heart.

They guided me all the day long to the mysteries of the country of pleasure and pain, and, at last, to what palace gate have they brought me in the evening at the end of my journey?

102

I BOASTED among men that I had known you. They see your pictures in all works of mine. They come and ask me, "Who is he?" I know not how to answer them. I say, "Indeed, I cannot tell." They blame me and they go away in scorn. And you sit there smiling.

I put my tales of you into lasting songs. The secret gushes out from my heart. They come and ask me, "Tell me all your meanings." I know not how to answer them. I say, "Ah, who knows what they mean!" They smile and go away in utter scorn. And you sit there smiling.

103

IN one salutation to thee, my God, let all my senses spread out and touch this world at thy feet.

Like a rain-cloud of July hung low with its burden of unshed showers let all my mind bend down at thy door in one salutation to thee.

Let all my songs gather together their diverse strains into a single current and flow to a sea of silence in one salutation to thee.

Like a flock of homesick cranes flying night and day back to their mountain nests let all my life take its voyage to its eternal home in one salutation to thee.

THESE translations are of poems contained in three books—Naivédya, Kheyá, and Gitánjali—to be had at the Indian Publishing House, 22 Cornwallis Street, Calcutta; and of a few poems which have appeared only in periodicals.

INDEX OF FIRST WORDS

THE END

PRINTED BY R. & R. CLARK, LTD., EDINBURGH